SHIH TZUS

by Allan Morey

Consultant: Jennifer Zablotny
Doctor of Veterinary Medicine
American Veterinary
Medical Association

Pebble® Plus

CAPSTONE PRESS
a capstone imprint

Pebble Plus is published by Capstone Press,
1710 Roe Crest Drive, North Mankato, Minnesota 56003
www.mycapstone.com

Library of Congress Cataloging-in-Publication Data
Names: Morey, Allan, author.
Title: Shih tzus / by Allan Morey.
Description: North Mankato, Minnesota : Capstone Press, [2017] | Series:
   Pebble Plus. Tiny dogs | Audience: Ages 4–7. | Audience: K to grade 3. |
   Includes bibliographical references and index.
Identifiers: LCCN 2016006873| ISBN 9781515719649 (library binding) | ISBN
   9781515719700 (ebook (pdf))
Subjects: LCSH: Shih tzu—Juvenile literature. | Toy dogs—Juvenile
   literature.
Classification: LCC SF429.S64 M67 2017 | DDC 636.76—dc23
LC record available at https://lccn.loc.gov/2016006873

Editorial Credits
Emily Raij, editor; Juliette Peters, designer;
Pam Mitsakos, media researcher; Laura Manthe, production specialist

Photo Credits
Getty Images: Anita Atta, 12–13; iStockphoto: Grant Shimmin, 7, Wilson Valentin, 21; Shutterstock:
Capture Light, 11, chaoss, 1, 4–5, kostolom3000, 3, back cover top left, Liliya Kulianionak, cover,
Pattarit S, 9, 19, vlastas, design element throughout book; Thinkstock: Costhin, 15,
PaaschPhotography, 17

Note to Parents and Teachers

The Tiny Dogs set supports national science standards related to life science. This book describes and illustrates shih tzus. The images support early readers in understanding the text. The repetition of words and phrases helps early readers learn new words. This book also introduces early readers to subject-specific vocabulary words, which are defined in the Glossary section. Early readers may need assistance to read some words and to use the Table of Contents, Glossary, Read More, Internet Sites, Critical Thinking Using the Common Core, and Index sections of the book.

Printed in the United States of America.
009656F16

TABLE OF CONTENTS

LION DOGS

Woof or roar? Shih tzus are dogs that look like little lions. Their name means "lion dog" in Chinese.

5

Shih tzus are an old dog breed.

The breed started in Tibet in Asia.

They were lap dogs for kings.

Today they make great
family pets.

SILKY, SWEET, AND STUBBORN

Shih tzus are small.

They are about the size

of a gallon of milk. They weigh

as much as two gallons of milk.

Shih tzus have long, flowing coats.

Their coats can be different colors.

Some are black, white, gray, or gold.

Their muzzle fur looks like a mustache.

Their tails curl up on their backs.

Shih tzus are friendly and playful.
They are good with other pets and
kids. Shih tzus do not bark a lot.

Shih tzus are not easy to train.

They can be stubborn.

They might not want to obey.

Shih tzus need patient owners.

SHIH TZUS AS PETS

Shih tzus need a lot of grooming.
They should be brushed
at least once a week.
Their fur needs to be trimmed
when it gets too long.

Shih tzus are indoor dogs.

They can get too hot in summer.

Their coats will not keep

them warm in winter.

Healthy shih tzus can live up to 16 years. They need more care than many other dogs. But they will reward you with lasting friendship!

GLOSSARY

reward—to give something for doing something well

breed—a certain kind of animal within an animal group

coat—an animal's hair or fur

groom—to clean and make an animal look neat

muzzle—an animal's nose, mouth, and jaws

obey—to do what someone tells you to do

stubborn—not willing to give in or change

train—to prepare for something by learning or practicing new skills

READ MORE

Gaines, Ann Graham. *Kids Top 10 Pet Dogs*. American Humane Association Top 10 Pets for Kids. Berkeley Heights, N.J.: Enslow Elementary, 2015.

Markovics, Joyce. *Shih Tzu: Lion Dog*. Little Dogs Rock! New York: Bearport, 2011.

Rustad, Martha E. H. *Dogs*. Smithsonian Little Scientist. North Mankato, Minn.: Capstone Press, 2015.

INTERNET SITES

FactHound offers a safe, fun way to find Internet sites related to this book. All of the sites on FactHound have been researched by our staff.

Here's all you do:

Visit *www.facthound.com*

Type in this code: 9781515719649

Check out projects, games and lots more at
www.capstonekids.com

CRITICAL THINKING USING THE COMMON CORE

1. What problems might you have if you had a pet shih tzu? How would you overcome these difficulties? (Integration of Knowledge and Ideas)

2. Why would you want a pet shih tzu? What do you like about this breed? (Integration of Knowledge and Ideas)

3. From reading this book, what are some things you learned that you need to do to take care of a pet? (Key Ideas and Details)

INDEX